C0-DBB-395

THE CATHOLIC SCHOOL PRINCIPAL:

AN OUTLINE FOR ACTION

Brother Theodore Drahmann, FSC
President
Christian Brothers College
Memphis, Tennessee

A Publication of the
National Catholic Educational Association

Copyright 1981
All Rights Reserved

PREFACE

In 1975 NCEA published a collection of essays under the title
The Principal's Toolbox: A Manual for Catholic Administrators,
edited by Fr. Emmet Harrington and Mary Glenzinski. It applied
certain principles and aspects of general school administration to
the Catholic school context. Much has changed and been learned
since then on this topic. It is with this change in mind that
NCEA recognized the need to publish a new text for this audience
written in such a manner so that it could be used in many diverse
learning contexts -- e.g., a new or experienced principal's in-
service program, a personal study program of profession development
undertaken by a principal, a college or university training program
for those interested in becoming principals in Catholic schools, etc.

The Catholic School Principal: An Outline for Action is such a
publication. It suggests those broad administrative contours with
which all Catholic school principals need to concern themselves.
The use of a checklist format along with issues that may be used for
discussion with many different groups suggests its practical nature.
It is not exhaustive, but certainly offers an overview of all those
basic areas which must be considered. It is produced in cooperation
with the NCEA Department of In-Service Programs.

The text is written by someone who has broad experience in the
area -- Brother Theodore Drahmann, F.S.C., President of Christian
Brothers College in Memphis, Tennessee. His Catholic school experience includes the positions of teacher, guidance counselor, and
principal in Chicago and Minnesota, as well as director of student
Christian Brothers and supervisor of schools for the Christian
Brothers. For six years he served as superintendent of elementary
and secondary schools for the Archdiocese of St. Paul and Minneapolis.
He was the first coordinator for the graduate program in nonpublic
school administration at the College of St. Thomas, St. Paul,
Minnesota. As the person who served as NCEA liaison with him and
coordinated this project, I want to express to him the appreciation
of NCEA and all those who will use this manual for the work he has
done.

I am also grateful to Kathleen T. Stief who typed the manuscript,
assisted with publishing details and to the Communications Committee
of NCEA who reviewed the material and made suggestions.

Bruno V. Manno, Ph.D.
Director, In-Service Programs and Data Bank
June, 1981

TABLE OF CONTENTS

1. INTRODUCTION

The Principal's Toolbox, edited by Fr. Emmet Harrington and Mary Glenzinski, and published by NCEA in 1975, has been a significant help in the renewal of leadership in Catholic schools and the revival of confidence among it administrators. The valuable articles in that publication touched on many of the principal areas of concern and interest for principals in the post-Vatican II Church, and helped to guide them through this difficult area of transition. A great debt of gratitude is due to the editors and to the authors who contributed the articles in the Toolbox.

But much has happened to Catholic schools since 1975. The present author's experience as a principal, as a supervisor for his religious community, as a diocesan superintendent of schools, and as a teacher of administration in a program designed for training private school administrators has led him to form a collection of "basics", that is, a listing of fundamental tasks which are the concern and responsibility of the leader of Catholic secondary and elementary schools. These were developed in conjunction with the principals of the archdiocesan schools in St. Paul and Minneapolis, as well as with his students in administration classes at the College of St. Thomas in St. Paul, Minnesota. Hopefully, they thus pass the test of reality and practicality, and possess the distinctiveness which characterizes the Catholic school system in the United States.

The Principal's Toolbox is a book of background reading, with generous helpings of "how-to-do-it" advice added to it. The present work, The Catholic School Principal: An Outline for Action, gives a specific overview of the tasks of the head of a Catholic elementary or secondary school in the form of checklists of items in the principal areas of responsibility.

A few words of explanation of the various sections of the following chapters may be useful to the readers.

Each section is introduced by a brief definition of the area and a description of the responsibility of the principal in that area. This is followed by a listing of the administrative actions to be taken by the principal, together with the season of the year in which that task is best done. In this section, as in the following, an asterisk (*) points out the priority items, actions that even the busiest teaching principal should not neglect. This is not to say that the remaining tasks are not important, but it merely recognized the fact that in the press of the school year, there is a limit to the time and energy of the principal, and choices must be made.

The second section (BOARD POLICIES AND ACTIONS) points out the specific decisions which belong to the board of education which helps to lead the school, and the recommended time for these actions. Since boards differ widely across the country, this section must be interpreted according to the degree of policy-making authority residing in the board.

The following divisions (FACULTY HANDBOOK and PARENT/STUDENT HANDBOOK) suggest topics which should be included in those publications for the information of the two groups indicated.

Section V (HELPFUL RESOURCES) attempts to list a few selected references which would be helpful for principals to gain further information in that area. Undoubtedly, there are many other publications available, but these have proved to be genuinely helpful aids to Catholic school principals; most of them are readily available through NCEA or other convenient sources. Write to NCEA for a complete list of NCEA publications as well as NCEA

Convention cassettes.

The final section (ISSUES) departs from the precise format of the foregoing sections, and points out the broad areas where Catholic school administration is indeed an art! These are broad questions of policy and action where there are no definite answers; educators will always be seeking to work out practical solutions to the problems they pose. However, principals should be aware of these issues and should try, in conjunction with their boards and/or staffs, to hammer out workable - if only tentative - solutions to guide them in the performance of their duties. Any one of these issues can well be the subject of workshops, faculty meetings, and board inservice sessions.

Readers will note that this publication is written in a checklist format. This is intended to help reduce the frustration level which often is the lot of a school principal. Manifold responsibilities tend to weigh upon the administrator, with the feeling that one's work is never done. Perhaps the opportunity to see a listing of specific tasks to be done, to decide which are to be done, and to have the satisfaction of checking them off when completed will serve to reduce this frustration. The checklist format is also intended to be an aid to beginning principals, so that they can have some assurance that they are covering the essential tasks included in their responsibilities. Experienced administrators may also find it useful as an "examination of conscience" to be sure that they are "covering all the bases", even though the author makes no claim to be complete and exhaustive in this publication.

Many individuals have contributed to this publication, and it would be impossible to name them all. The author is particularly indebted to his

colleagues in the National Catholic Educational Association, especially the
Washington staff and his fellow administrators in the department of Chief
Administrators of Catholic Education (CACE), to his conferreres on the
National Education Council of the Christian Brothers, and to his student and
faculty colleagues in the NEW DESIGN FOR SCHOOL LEADERSHIP program in nonpublic school administration at the College of St. Thomas in St. Paul with
whom he served before accepting his position in Memphis. A special word of
tribute is due to the warm and supportive group of principals of Catholic
grade and high schools in the Archdiocese of St. Paul and Minneapolis, whom
he had the privilege of serving for six years as superintendent.

Brother Theodore Drahmann, FSC
President
Christian Brothers College
Memphis, Tennessee

2. THE PRINCIPAL AS LEADER

The principal is the key to a quality school. The quality of a principal's leadership is affected by the vision, knowledge, competence, and personal qualities of the person who holds that position. The principal's leadership is a blend of managerial skill and the dynamism which is able to move others to perform well and to grow. These qualities may be as diverse as are the human beings who possess them; however, the following items provide a listing of basic tasks and responsibilities which should be carried out by all principals.

I. <u>Administrative Actions to Take</u>   <u>Season</u>

    *_____1. Has a clear, specific job description

    *_____2. Knows and communicates with superiors and other educational leaders in the area

    _____3. Is aware of one's leadership style

    _____4. Seeks regular evaluation from board and staff   Winter

    _____5. Has an annual program of personal and professional improvement (retreats, courses, workshops, conventions, etc.)

    _____6. Is a member of a professional administrator's organization; attends its meetings

    _____7. Reads some professional literature regularly

II. <u>Board Policies and Decisions</u>

    *_____1. Hires principal   Winter

    *_____2. Clarifies relationship with principal   Winter

    *_____3. Approves principal's job description   Winter

    _____4. Evaluates principal annually   Winter

III. Faculty Handbook

*_____ 1. Contains administrators' job description

*_____ 2. States the educational and Church authorities to
which the school is accountable (Board, Supt.,
Bishop, etc.)

*_____ 3. Clarifies decision-making procedures in the school

_____ 4. Contains appropriate excerpts from and references
to major statements by educational and Church leaders

_____ 5. Refers to major sources of research regarding current
educational practice

IV. Parent/Student Handbook

*_____ 1. Outlines authority structure in the school
(Board, Supt., principal, etc.)

*_____ 2. Notes the educational and Church authorities to
which the school is accountable

_____ 3. Contains excerpts from and references to appropriate
major statements of educational and Church leaders

V. Helpful Resources

_____ 1. State Department of Education publications and
personnel

_____ 2. District supervisors

_____ 3. Journals and publications from:
American Association of School Administrators
Association for Supervision and Curriculum Development
National and State Elementary Principals Associations
Phi Delta Kappa

_____ 4. Eleim, Stanley (ed). A Decade of Gallup Polls of Attitudes
Toward Education, Bloomington, IN: Phi Delta Kappa, 1978.
(See also annual surveys published each year in Phi Delta
Kappan.)

_____ 5. Administrator Perceiver (Selection Research, Inc., 2546
South 48th, P.O. Box 6438, Lincoln, NE 68506)

_____ 6. Diocesan Principals' Handbooks

_____7. <u>Doctoral Dissertations on Catholic Education 1968-1975</u>.
Washington, DC: National Catholic Educational Association, 1975

_____8. Glenzinski, Mary and Harrington, Emmet, <u>The Principal's
Toolbox</u>. Washington, D.C.: National Catholic Educational
Association, 1975.

_____9. Greeley, Andrew, <u>Catholic Schools in a Declining Church</u>.
Kansas City: Sheed and Ward, 1976

_____10. <u>Media and Catechetics Today</u>. Washington, D.C.: National
Catholic Educational Association, 1980

_____11. Publications of the National Catholic Educational Association
(<u>Momentum</u>, <u>Alive</u>, <u>NCEA Notes</u>, etc.)

_____12. National Conference of Catholic Bishops. <u>To Teach as Jesus
Did</u>. Washington, D.C.: United States Catholic Conference, 1973

_____13. Sacred Congregations for Catholic Education. <u>The Catholic
School</u>. Washington, D.C.: United States Catholic Conference,
1977

_____14. <u>Sharing the Light of Faith: National Catechetical Directory</u>.
Washington, D.C.: United States Catholic Conference, 1979

_____15. <u>Should We Be More Assertive About Our Christian Values?</u>
Washington, D.C.: National Catholic Educational Association,
1974

_____16. <u>Today's Catholic Teacher</u>. (Monthly). Dayton, Ohio: Peter Li, Inc.

VI. <u>Issues</u>

_____1. Is the principal a manager or leader?

_____2. What should a principal read?

_____3. How much freedom of action should a principal have?

_____4. How should a principal be accountable? To whom?

_____5. To what extent are leaders "born", to what extent are they
"made"?

_____6. What is the ideal relationship between principal and board?

_____7. What are the essential qualities of an effective principal?

3. THE PRINCIPAL AS RELIGIOUS LEADER

The principal of a religious school has unique leadership responsibilites with regard to the life and growth of the faculty and students of that school. The principal must be a person of faith and attachment to Christ, loyal to the Church, and possess a general understanding of the process of religious growth. There must be a grasp of the content and methods of religious instruction, together with a knowledge of current resources for teachers and students. The ability to inspire and unify the faculty with regard to the religious mission of the school must also be present.

I. Administrative Actions to Take   Season

_____1.	Prepares (or revises) a school philosophy with specific religious elements	Fall
*_____2.	Hires teachers who can contribute to the religious mission of the school	Spring
_____3.	Provides teacher inservice for faith growth	
*_____4.	Supervises religion curriculum and texts	
*_____5.	Schedules liturgy, retreats, and prayer experiences for staff and students	Fall
*_____6.	Hires religion teachers who are adequately prepared	Spring
_____7.	Schedules the parish clergy into the life of the school	Fall
_____8.	Publicizes and explains the religion program	Fall
_____9.	Schedules the special components of a religious growth program:	Fall
*_____	a. Sacramental preparation	
_____	b. Christian service program	
_____	c. Family life program	

_____ d. Vocations program

_____ e. Social justice

_____10. Seclects appropriate evaluation tools

_____11. Has a process for aiding teachers to integrate religious principles into the curriculum

II. Board Policies and Decisions

* _____ 1. Sets faculty religious qualifications

* _____ 2. Sets policy for non-Catholic teachers and students

* _____ 3. Approves family life program

III. Faculty Handbook

* _____ 1. Religious expectations of faculty

* _____ 2. Calendar of religious activities and inservice

_____ 3. Class prayer policy

_____ 4. Summary of religion program

IV. Parent/Student Handbook

_____ 1. Summary of religion program

_____ 2. Summary of special programs:

_____ a. Sacramental preparation

_____ b. Family life

_____ c. Christian service

_____ d. Liturgies and prayers

V. Helpful Resources

_____1. Barrett, Msgr. Francis X., and Olsen, Bro. John D. Guidelines for Selected Personnel Practices in Catholic Schools: Parts I and II. Washington, D.C.: National Catholic Educational Association, 1975

_____2. Catechists Never Stop Learning. Washington, D.C.: National Catholic Educational Association, 1972

_____3. Catholic Education: An Overall View. Washington, D.C.: National Catholic Educational Association, cassette

_____4. Contemporary Issues in Catholic High Schools. Washington, D.C.: National Catholic Educational Association, 1981

_____5. Catholic Schools in America. Washington, D.C.: National Catholic Educational Association and Englewood, CO: Fisher Publishing Co., published yearly

_____6. Faith Community. Washington, D.C.: National Catholic Educational Association, cassette

_____7. Gilmour, Peter. Praying Together. Winona, MN: St. Mary's College Press, 1978

_____8. Giving Form to the Vision: The Pastoral in Practice. Washington, D.C.: National Catholic Educational Association, 1974 (Available in four sections: Adult, Elementary, Secondary, Policy-Making)

_____9. Hear the Word, Share the Word, Guide Your People. Washington, D.C.: National Catholic Educational Association, 1978

_____10. Hennessy, Sister Rose Marie, OP. The Principal as Prophet. Washington, D.C.: National Catholic Educational Association, 1978

_____11. I Believe in God. Washington, D.C.: National Catholic Educational Association, 1975

_____12. McBride, Rev. Alfred. Evangelization: The Mission and Ministry of Catholic Educators. Washington, D.C.: National Conference of Directors of Religious Education, 1978

_____13. National Conference of Catholic Bishops. To Teach As Jesus Did. Washington, D.C.: United States Catholic Conference, 1973

_____14. Qualities and Competencies of the Religion Teacher. Washington, D.C.: National Conference of Directors of Religious Education, 1973

_____15. Publications of the National Catholic Educational Association (Momentum, Alive, NCEA Notes, etc.)

_____16. Sacred Congregation for Catholic Education. The Catholic School. Washington, D.C.: United States Catholic Conference, 1977

_____17. Sharing the Light of Faith: National Catechetical Directory. Washington, D.C.: United States Catholic Conference, 1979

_____18. Smith, Thomas. Religious Education Requirements and Recommendations for Teaching Personnel in Catholic Elementary Schools. Washington, D.C.: National Catholic Educational Association, 1978

_____19. Today's Catholic Teacher. (Monthly). Dayton, Ohio: Peter Li, Inc.

_____20. Van Merrienboer, Edward, et al. Seeking a Just Society: An Educational Design. Washington, D.C.: National Catholic Educational Association, 1978

_____21. What Makes A Catholic School Catholic? Washington, D.C.: National Catholic Educational Association, cassette

VI. Issues

_____1. How "holy" must a principal be?

_____2. Should a parish school principal belong to that parish?

_____3. Should non-Catholics be hired to teach in a Catholic school?

_____4. What is the relationship between a teacher's personal religious life and his/her role in a religious school?

_____5. How does one balance content and experience in the religious instruction program?

_____6. Should Mass attendance be required?

_____7. What is an effective program in Christian sexuality which is acceptable to parents?

_____8. How can Christian social principles be properly included in the life and the curriculum of the school?

_____9. How does one develop a consensus among faculty of varying religious philosophies (e.g., liberal, conservative)?

4. THE PRINCIPAL AS LEADER OF FACULTY AND STAFF

The principal is the leader of the adult community of faculty and staff which serves the student body of the school. This is in many respects the most significant aspect of the role of the principal, since it is the adults in the school who most directly affect the students and are responsible for the growth of these young folk for whom the school exists. As leader, the principal has responsibilities for employment procedures, faculty and staff communication and morale, as well as in-service. The principal also acts as the liaison between the faculty and staff with the board, pastor, parents, and the community outside the school.

I. Administrative Actions to Take   Season

    *_____1. Recruits, interviews, hires teachers   Spring

    *_____2. Orients new faculty   Summer

    *_____3. Supervises and evaluates teachers and staff

    *_____4. Recommends contract renewals and dismissals Spring

    *_____5. Publishes (revises) faculty handbook   Summer

    *_____6. Schedules faculty meetings   Fall

    *_____7. Provides faculty inservice

II. Board Policies and Actions

    *_____1. Sets teacher qualifications

    *_____2. Publishes an appeal process for grievances

    *_____3. Adopts personnel policies

    *_____4. Sets salary schedule and fringe benefits   Winter

    *_____5. Approves contracts, dismissals   Spring

III. Faculty Handbook

    * _____ 1. Personnel policies

    * _____ 2. Salary schedule and fringe benefits

    * _____ 3. Evaluation procedures

    * _____ 4. Grievance procedures

    * _____ 5. Contract dates

IV. Parent/Student Handbook

    _____ 1. List of teachers

    * _____ 2. Procedure for contacting teachers

V. Helpful Resources

    _____ 1. Augenstein, John J. A Collaborative Approach to Personnel Relations. Washington, D.C.: National Catholic Educational Association, 1980

    _____ 2. Barrett, Msgr. Francis X., Olsen, Bro. John D. Guidelines for Selected Personnel Practices in Catholic Schools, Part I. Washington, D.C.: National Catholic Educational Association, 1975

    _____ 3. Harrington, Rev. Emmet, and Glenzinski, Mary. The Principal's Toolbox. Washington, D.C.: National Catholic Educational Association, 1975

    _____ 4. Quality Selection Process, a guide for recruitment, interviews, hiring and orientation of teachers for Catholic schools (Toledo Catholic Educational Services, 436 W. Delaware, Toledo, OH 43610)

    _____ 5. Sharing the Light of Faith: National Catechetical Directory. Washington, D.C.: United States Catholic Conference, 1979. Chapter 9

    _____ 6. Selection Research, Inc. (2546 South 48th, P.O. Box 6438, Lincoln, NE 68506) has developed a structured interview process of identifying applicants with desirable teacher qualities.

    _____ 7. Teacher As Minister Daily Plan Book. Washington, D.C. : National Catholic Educational Association, published yearly

_____8. <u>Unionism in Catholic Schools</u>. Washington, D.C.: National Catholic Educational Association, 1976

VI. <u>Issues</u>

_____1. How can <u>good</u> teachers be identified?

_____2. What is a fair process for dismissing a teacher?

_____3. What is the point where a poor teacher must be dismissed to assure the right of students to good education?

_____4. How can a grievance procedure be best carried out?

_____5. What should a principal do about teachers involved in objectionable life styles or practices: invalid marriages, gay, abortion, drugs, etc.?

_____6. What is the place of unions in Catholic schools?

5. THE PRINCIPAL AS CURRICULUM LEADER

The principal's role as educational leader is the key to the successful operation of the school. Along with his/her work in the areas of selection, supervision, and inservice of faculty, the management of the school curriculum is crucial to the task of educational leadership as such. Although the principal may delegate curriculum matters to other administrators, department chairpersons, and individual faculty members, it remains true that final responsibility for the instructional process remains with the head of the school.

I. **Administrative Actions to Take**   Season

    * _____ 1. Knows the scope and sequence of the present curriculum

    * _____ 2. Reviews curriculum in relation to school philosophy and needs of present students   Spring

    * _____ 3. Reviews curriculum in terms of faculty expertise and present schedule   Spring

    _____ 4. Appoints curriculum coordinators and committees as needed and suitable to the school   Summer

    * _____ 5. Involves faculty in materials selected and purchased   Spring

    _____ 6. Coordinates curriculum with high schools to be attended by present students (or) by feeder grade schools

    _____ 7. Reviews teacher lesson plans as needed

    * _____ 8. Provides for continual curriculum evaluation and revision

    _____ 9. Keeps abreast of general curriculum trends

    * _____ 10. Provides for integration of Christian principles into the curriculum

II. Board Policies and Decisions

      _____1. Is informed by principal of school curriculum in general

      _____2. May be asked to approve significant curriculum changes

    *_____3. May be asked to approve curriculum in sensitive areas: religion program, Christian sexuality

III. Faculty Handbook

    *_____1. Responsibilities for implementing present curriculum

      _____2. Responsibilities for evaluation, revision, and development of curriculum

      _____3. Philosophy and general outline of the school curriculum

      _____4. Recommended resources and professional memberships

    *_____5. Procedures for selection and purchase of curriculum materials

      _____6. Inventories of equipment, AV materials, etc.

IV. Parent/Student Handbook

      _____1. Philosophy, purposes, scope, and sequence of school curriculum

    *_____2. Listing of textbooks in use

      _____3. Procedure for parent involvement and input into curriculum

V. Helpful Resources

      _____1. Vision and Values in the Catholic School (entitled Toward A Catholic Value-Oriented Curriculum during the pilot of the project). Information available through NCEA or Grolier Educational Services, 707 Westchester Avenue, White Plains, NY 10604

_____2. Diocesan curriculum guides

_____3. Periodicals:

_____   a. Momentum

_____   b. Today's Catholic Teacher

_____4. Local college curriculum specialists and diocesan
         supervisors

_____5. Textbook publisher representatives

_____6. State departments of education and local public
         school curriculum specialists

_____7. Journals and other publications of the following associations:
         Association for Supervision and Curriculum Development
         State and National Principals' Associations
         American Association of School Administrators
         Phi Delta Kappa

_____8. Coping with Doctrinal Development. Washington, D.C.: National
         Catholic Educational Association, cassettes

_____9. Curriculum Guide for Health Education: Nutrition. Washington,
         D.C.: National Catholic Educational Association, 1975

_____10. Differentiated Patterns of Education in Catholic Elementary
         Schools. Washington, D.C.: National Catholic Educational
         Association, 1973

_____11. Directory of Catholic Special Facilities and Programs in the
         US for Handicapped Children and Adults. Washington, D.C.:
         National Catholic Educational Association, 1979

_____12. Focus on American Catechetics: A Commentary on the General
         Catechetical Directory. Washington, D.C.: National Catholic
         Educational Association, 1972

_____13. How to Teach Christian Morality. Washington, D.C.: National
         Catholic Educational Association and Catholic Television
         Network TV Video Cassettes

_____14. Individualized Instruction for What? Washington, D.C.: National
         Catholic Educational Association, cassette

_____15. Recognizing and Helping the Learning Disabled Child in Your
         Classroom. Washington, D.C.: National Catholic Educational
         Association, 1978

_____16. Sharing the Light of Faith - The National Catechetical Directory.
         Washington, D.C.: NCEA and Catholic Television Network Video
         Cassettes

VI. Issues

_____1. How can Catholic Christian principles be truly integrated into the entire curriculum?

_____2. To what degree should schools go "back to the basics"?

_____3. How broadly should we understand the term "curriculum"?

_____4. Should curriculum be tightly planned and structured in the form of specific activities, or should it be laid out as a framework from which many types of experiences are possible?

_____5. How much should a principal "control" the curriculum?

_____6. Is integration between the curriculum of grade schools and high schools possible?

_____7. What is a "quality curriculum"?

_____8. How can a principal be both the building administrator and the curriculum manager?

_____9. When cutting curriculum programs, how are priorities determined?

6. THE PRINCIPAL AS PUPIL MANAGER

The principal has overall responsibility for the life of the school and for the general welfare of the students who attend. These responsibilities include traditional matters such as attendance, discipline, health, safety, and playground supervision, as well as more contemporary problems resulting from family disorders, drug abuse, and growing legal restrictions.

I. <u>Administrative Actions to Take</u>   <u>Season</u>

*_____1. Set absence and tardiness procedures   Fall

_____2. Establish and review a discipline policy   Fall

_____3. Establish and review a homework policy   Fall

*_____4. Select grading and reporting procedures   Spring

_____5. Establish and maintain dress guidelines   Spring

*_____6. Provide for hallway, lunchroom, and play-
          ground supervision   Fall

_____7. Provide a policy on drug abuse and smoking   Fall

_____8. Provide counseling and guidance services

*_____9. Provide health services and procedures

*____10. Know referral agencies for problems which
          the school cannot solve

*____11. Maintain adequate records

____12. Establish procedures for suspension,
          expulsion, promotion and non-promotion   Fall

II. <u>Board Policies and Actions</u>

*_____1. Sets age of admission

*_____2. Adopts a policy of non-discrimination in
          admission

_____3. Sets policy on dress guidelines

_____4. Approves a grievance process for students

III. Faculty Handbook

*_____1. Discipline policy and procedures

*_____2. Homework policy

*_____3. Tardiness and absence procedures

*_____4. Playground and lunchroom duties

*_____5. Policy on drugs, alcohol, and smoking

_____6. Uniform regulations, enforcement

IV. Parent/Student Handbook

*_____1. Attendance procedures

*_____2. Discipline policy and procedures

*_____3. Homework expectations

*_____4. Special regulations: drugs, alcohol, smoking

*_____5. Uniform regulations

_____6. Promotion and non-promotion policies

V. Helpful Resources

_____1. Student As Diciple Complete Kit. Washington, D.C.: National Catholic Educational Association, 1980

_____2. Creating an Early Learning Center in an Unused Building. Washington, D.C.: National Catholic Educational Association, 1972

VI. Issues

_____ 1. What is a fair and effective policy on:

_____   a. homework?

_____   b. discipline?

_____   c. attendance?

_____ 2. How long should a Catholic school retain students who are serious discipline problems?

_____ 3. When can conduct outside school affect a student's status in a Catholic school?

_____ 4. How can students with drug and alcohol problems best be helped?

_____ 5. Should the teachers or the principal handle discipline problems?

_____ 6. Is corporal punishment suitable in Catholic schools?

_____ 7. How can teachers with poor contol over their classrooms be aided?

_____ 8. How can a principal ensure the enforcement of school rules by all teachers?

7. THE PRINCIPAL AS FINANCIAL LEADER

In all schools the principal has specific financial responsibility, although the scope may differ according to the extent to which others share that responsibility, i.e., board, pastor, parish finance committee. The listing below indicates a rather complete listing of the financial duties of the head of a Catholic school; the principal must at least be aware that these are to be done by others if not by him/herself. It is evident that there be a wise use of financial resources and an accurate, clear accounting for them.

I. Administrative Actions to Take

	Season
*_____1. Initiate the budget-planning process	Winter
*_____2. See that tuition, salary, and other budget decisions are made	Winter
*_____3. Provide regular financial reports to board	
*_____4. Ensure careful financial record-keeping	
*_____5. Ensure prompt tuition collections	
*_____6. Ensure prompt payment of outstanding bills	
_____7. Arrange for investment of surplus school funds on a short-term or long-term basis	
_____8. Organize fund-raising program	Spring
_____9. Provide for budget revision	Spring, Fall
*_____10. Control the budget	
_____11. Give annual financial report to parents	Spring (or) Fall
_____12. Provide scholarship funds to aid needy students	
_____13. Involve staff in budget-planning	Winter
_____14. Publicize scholarship opportunities	Spring

22

_____15. Develop a long-range financial plan

II. Board Policies and Decisions

    *_____1. Approve tuition, salaries, benefits, and
            budget   Spring

    _____2. Approve collection policy of overdue tuition

    _____3. Approve fund-raising program   Spring

    *_____4. Approve final financial statement for
            previous year   Fall

    *_____5. Work with principal (through finance committee)
            in development of budget   Winter,
                                                    Spring

III. Faculty Handbook

    *_____1. Salary schedule, benefits, pay periods,
            deductions

    *_____2. Purchase authorization and purchase
            procedures

    _____3. Summary of school budget and financial
            report

    _____4. Staff involvement in budget-planning process

    _____5. Tuition policy for children of faculty and
            staff

    *_____6. Policy on classroom collections and sale of
            materials to children

    *_____7. Process for approving the imposition of
            additional financial requirements on students
            by individual teachers, e.g., requiring the
            purchase of special materials, additional
            books

IV. Parent/Student Handbook

*_____1. Tuition and fee schedule and payment plans

_____2. School financial report

_____3. Scholarship opportunities

_____4. School fund-raising program

V. Resources

_____1. NCEA Data Bank. Catholic Elementary Schools and Their
         Finances 1980. Washington, D.C.: National Catholic Educational
         Association, 1980. Issued annually or bi-annually

_____2. NCEA Data Bank. Catholic Secondary Schools and Their
         Finances 1980. Washington, D.C.: National Catholic Educational
         Association, 1980. Issued annually or bi-annually

_____3. Harrington, Rev. Emmet, and Glenzinski, Mary. The Principal's
         Toolbox. Washington, D.C.: National Catholic Educational
         Association, 1975

_____4. National Conference on Catholic School Finance. (Proceedings
         of the 1974, 1975, and 1977 conferences) Washington, D.C.:
         National Catholic Educational Association

_____5. Accounting Manual for Catholic Elementary and Secondary Schools.
         Washington, D.C.: National Catholic Educational Association,
         1969

_____6. Moroni, Bro. J. Alfred, FSC. An Accounting Manual for
         Elementary and Secondary Schools. Washington, D.C.: National
         Catholic Educational Association, 1969

_____7. Catholic School Management Newsletter. 24 Cornfield Lane,
         Madison, Connecticut 06443

_____8. Accounting for Independent Schools. Boston, MA: National
         Association of Independent Schools, 1969

VI. Issues

_____1. How much tuition can Catholic parents afford to pay?

_____2. What is the ideal "mix" of parish subsidy and
           student tuition?

_____3. What are effective and appropriate fund-raising
           projects for Catholic schools?

_____4. Should Catholic schools have development directors?

_____5. Should Catholic schools be completely self-supporting
           (no parish or diocesan subsidy)?

_____6. How can and should inner city Catholic schools be
           financed?

_____7. What is a "just wage" for Catholic school teachers?

_____8. What will be the effect of continuing high inflation
           on the future of Catholic schools?

_____9. How are priorities established when budget cuts are
           to be made?

_____10. How should parish funds for education be divided between
           the school and the non-school programs?

_____11. What is the best working relationship between the
           principal and the board's finance committee? Between the
           board and the parish finance committee and/or parish
           council in budgetary matters?

8. THE PRINCIPAL AND THE SCHOOL PHILOSOPHY

Each school should have a written statement of its philosophy, including the beliefs, values, goals, and objectives that inspire its educational programs. The statement should express the identity of the religious school and the views of the staff and parents regarding the means which help human and religious growth, the nature of learning, the setting for learning, and citizenship in our nation.

I. Administrative Actions to Take	Season
*_____1. Adopt a process for formulating (or updating) the school philosophy	Spring
*_____2. Use the philosophy when hiring, orienting, and evaluating staff	
*_____3. Publish the philosophy to the pastor, staff, board, parents, parish, and students	Fall
_____4. Review the philosophy yearly with the faculty	Fall

II. Board Policies and Actions	
*_____1. Require a philosophy statement	
*_____2. Approve the philosophy statement	
_____3. Review the philosophy statement annually	Fall

III. Faculty Handbook	
*_____1. Statement of philosophy	
_____2. Expectations regarding the philosophy	

IV. Parent/Student Handbook

    *_____1. Brief, simple version of philosophy statement

V. Helpful Resources

The following publications will be of help in the process of formulatling a school philosophy statement.

For assistance in determining the content, it is recommended that the major contemporary documents on Catholic education be consulted: To Teach As Jesus Did, The Catholic School, Sharing the Light of Faith.

    *_____1. Harrington, Rev. Emmet, and Glenzinski, Mary. The Principal's Toolbox. Washington, D.C.: National Catholic Educational Association, 1975

    _____2. Giving Form to the Vision. Washington, D.C.: National Catholic Educational Association, 1974. Available in four sections: Adult, Elementary, Secondary, Policy-Making

VI. Issues

    _____1. Does a philosophy statement make a difference? Can it?

    _____2. How much consensus is needed among a staff regarding the philosophy statement?

    _____3. Should a philosophy statement include goals, objectives, and programs?

    _____4. How much should parents, board, and/or students be involved in the process of forming (or revising) a philosophy statement?

    _____5. How can the philosophy statement be helpful when hiring new teachers?

9. THE PRINCIPAL AND BOARDS OF EDUCATION

It has been said that one of the prime duties of a Catholic school principal today is the "care and feeding" of the board of education. Because boards are rather new in the operation of Catholic schools, this responsibility is not always recognized. Yet it is increasingly true that the leadership of Catholic education must be shared with parents and the broader community through the medium of boards of education. Such would be an authentic living out of the teachings of Vatican II regarding collegiality and shared decision-making.

The respective roles of principal and board members are often not clearly defined, and there must be continuing effort to spell out the areas proper to each. In this regard, it may be helpful to note that the principal is the leader of the board (initiator of educational policy); the teacher of the board (guides board development and furnishes necessary information); the motivator of the board (inspires and challenges board members to growth in a sense of the mission of Catholic education); and - where the board has final policy decisions - the employee of the board.

I. Administrative Actions to Take   Season

    *_____ 1. Begin a board if one is lacking

    _____ 2. Provide in-service for the board

    *_____ 3. Present policy matters for action by the board

    *_____ 4. Provide regular information on school matters to the board

    *_____ 5. Assist in agenda preparation for board meetings

    *_____ 6. Present regular financial statements to the board

*_____7. Assist in the preparation of the annual
board calendar   Summer

_____8. Provide for orientation of new board members   Summer

*_____9. Recommend school personnel for hiring   Spring

II. Board Policies and Decisions

_____1. Review constitution and policies annually   Fall

_____2. Adopt regular program of board in-service   Fall

_____3. Consider membership in the National Association
of Boards of Education (NABE) - NCEA   Fall

*_____4. Hire and evaluate the principal   Winter

*_____5. Clarify relationship to parish council, to
parent association, to pastor, to diocesan
education office, and to diocesan board of
education

_____6. Conduct annual evaluation of itself   Spring

III. Faculty Handbook

*_____1. Nature, authority, and membership of board

*_____2. Relationship of faculty to the board
(teacher observer)

*_____3. Board policies which affect the faculty

*_____4. Grievance procedure for appeal to the board

IV. Parent/Student Handbook

*_____1. Nature, authority, and membership of the board

*_____2. Procedure for parent communication with the
board

*_____3. Election procedures

*_____4. Date, time, location of board meetings

*_____5. Distinctive roles of pastor, principal,
        council, board, and parents association

V. Resources

_____1. <u>Achieving Shared Reponsibility in the American Church</u>.
        Washington, D.C.: National Catholic Educational Association, 1977

_____2. <u>An In-Service Program for Catholic Education Boards</u>. Audiotapes
        and videotapes, narrated by Sr. Mary Benet McKinney, OSB.
        Washington, D.C.: National Association of Boards of Education
        (NCEA)

_____3. <u>Board Manual for Catholic Schools and Religious Education Programs</u>.
        Spokane, Washington: Office of Education and Religious Education

_____4. <u>Giving Form to the Vision: Education Policy-Making</u>. Washington,
        D.C.: National Catholic Educational Association. Available in
        four sections: Adult, Elementary, Secondary, Policy-Making

_____5. Glenzinski, Mary, and Harrington, Rev. Emmet. <u>The Principal's
        Toolbox</u>. Washington, D.C.: National Catholic Educational
        Association, 1975

_____6. Harper, Mary Angela. <u>Ascent to Excellence in Catholic Education:
        A Guide to Effective Decision-Making</u>. Washington, D.C.: National
        Association of Boards of Education, 1980

_____7. Harper, Mary Angela. <u>Putting It All Together</u>. Washington, D.C.:
        National Association of Boards of Education, 1979

_____8. <u>Let Peace and Justice Prevail</u>. Washington, D.C.: National
        Catholic Educational Association, 1980

_____9. McKinney, Sr. Mary Benet, OSB. <u>Shared Decision-Making Revisited</u>.
        Chicago: Archdiocese of Chicago School Office, 1977

____10. Murdick, Olin, and Meyers, John F. <u>Boards of Education: A Primer</u>.
        Washington, D.C.: National Association of Boards of Education
        (NCEA)

____11. O'Brien, Rev. J. Stephen, ed. <u>The Parish: What Makes It Work</u>?
        Huntington, IN: Our Sunday Visitor and Washington, D.C.,
        National Catholic Educational Association, 1980

_____12. Policy-Maker. Newsletter published by the National Association of Boards of Education, One Dupont Circle, Suite 350, Washington, D.C. 20036

VI. Issues

_____1. How can the distinction between policy and administration be clearly understood?

_____2. How can a board attract quality members?

_____3. How can factions within a board be avoided?

_____4. How can a trusting, open relationship between board and principal be built?

_____5. How can a board have effective meetings?

_____6. What is the pastor's relationship with the board?

_____7. Should boards be appointed or elected?

_____8. How can a sense of Christian community be developed in a board?

_____9. How can a good relationship between the board and the parish council, and with the parent association, be best developed?

_____10. How can a board develop a sense of mission regarding Catholic education?

10. THE PRINCIPAL AND PARENTS

It is an accepted fact in both Church teaching and American law that parents are the "primary educators" of their children, and that the school and other educational agencies exist to assist them in their task. For this reason, it is important that principals of Catholic schools have a clear idea of the extent to which parents are to be involved in the operation of the school, through communication, consultation, activities, and decision-making. The more this collaboration takes place, the more both family and school will develop a helping relationship characterized by mutual support and invitations to each other to grow.

I. Administrative Actions to Take   Season

    *_____1. Encourage the organization and maintenance of a parent association

    *_____2. Plan regular parent communication procedures (newsletters, letters, open house, parent-teacher conferences)   Spring

    _____3. Organize a volunteer program to invite parent assistance and involvement in the school

    _____4. Produce a Parent Handbook with the assistance of parents   Fall

    _____5. Publicly recognize parent volunteers on a regular basis   Spring

II. Board Policies and Decisions

    *_____1. Provide for on-going communication and liaison with parent association

    *_____2. Provide for representation from parent association officers at board meetings

III. Faculty Handbook

    _____1. Policy regarding the role of parents in this
              school educational program

  *_____2. Parent-teacher conferences schedule and procedures

  *_____3. Policy on handling parent complaints

  *_____4. Nature, role, and schedule of parent association:
              teacher involvement and expectations

    _____5. Teacher involvement with parent volunteers:
              duties, limitations

IV. Parent/Student Handbook

  *_____1. Nature, organization, schedule of parent association

  *_____2. Schedule of parent-teacher conferences and report
              cards

    _____3. Description of parent volunteer program

V. Resources

    _____1. Diocesan office

    _____2. Local parent association

    _____3. National Forum for Catholic Parent Organizations
              (Suite 350, One Dupont Circle, Washington, D.C. 20036)

    _____4. Catholic Parent Organizations Program Guidebook and
              Catholic Parent Organizations Handbook. Washington, D.C.:
              National Catholic Educational Association, 1976

VI. Issues

    _____1. How can parents be genuinely involved in the education of
              their children without infringing upon the proper perogatives
              of professional educators?

_____2. What are effective programs for parent associations?

_____3. To what extent should Catholic schools try to serve the needs of families as such, over and beyond the education of their children?

_____4. How can volunteers be utilized for maximum benefit to school and faculty, avoiding interference by them in the internal affairs of the school while providing for suggestions and insights from them?

11. THE PRINCIPAL AND CHURCH AUTHORITIES

The Catholic school principal is a "minister" of the Church. He/she serves as one of the most important leaders of the Church's enterprise and must work in cordial collaboration with hierarchical Church leaders and with leaders of other ministries. The nature of relationships may differ according to the type of school served, e.g., parish, diocesan, regional, or private.

I. Administrative Actions to Take   Season

* _____ 1. Clarify the job description of the principal
            as a member of the staff   Fall

* _____ 2. Clarify the policies for use of school
            facilities by other parish groups   Summer

  _____ 3. Determine the involvement of the principal
            in other parish activities

  _____ 4. Schedule the involvement of the parish
            clergy in the activities of the school   Fall

* _____ 5. Set up regular patterns of communication
            with pastor(s) and other church authorities

  _____ 6. Include parish and diocesan events in the
            yearly school calendar   Summer

II. Board Policies

* _____ 1. Use of school facilities by parish and
            non-parish groups   Summer

  _____ 2. Relationship to appropriate parish and
            diocesan authorities

III. Faculty Handbook

* _____ 1. Relationship to the parish, the diocese,
            the Church

_____2. Faculty responsibilities to the local
parish(es)

_____3. Use of school facilities by other parish
groups

IV. Parent/Student Handbook

*_____1. Relationship of the school to the parish,
the diocese, the Church

_____2. Participation of students in parish activities

V. Helpful Resources

_____1. Directory/Department of Chief Administrators of
Catholic Education (CACE). Washington, D.C.: National
Catholic Educational Association, published yearly

_____2. Harrington, Rev. Emmet, and Glenzinski, Mary. The Principal's
Toolbox. Washington, D.C.: National Catholic Educational
Association, 1975

_____3. O'Brien, Rev. J. Stephen, ed. The Parish: What Makes It Work?
Huntington, IN: Our Sunday Visitor and Washington, D.C.,
National Catholic Educational Association, 1980

_____4. Sharing the Light of Faith: National Catechetical Directory.
Washington, D.C.: United States Catholic Conference, 1979

VI. Issues

_____1. To what extent should a principal be involved in parish
activities?

_____2. How can the parish clergy be best involved in the school?

_____3. How can the principal minimize the problems which often
arise when school facilities are used for other parish
activities?

_____4. How can significant parish and diocesan events be included
in the school program?

_____5. How can tension between the school and non-school personnel in the parish be eliminated?

_____6. To what extent is the concept of "total Catholic education" in a parish feasible?

_____7. How can Catholic high schools maintain good relations with the parishes which supply them with students?

12. THE PRINCIPAL AND RELIGIOUS ORDERS

Most Catholic schools include members of religious orders among their staff and/or in administrative positions. The continuing value of religious teachers, as well as the unique contributions they make to Catholic schools, should be recognized by the principal, whether he/she be religious or lay. There should be an awareness of the responsibility of the principal regarding the members of religious orders who serve on the staff of the school.

I. Administrative Actions to Take   Season

* _____ 1. Clarify contractual agreements and/or
              placement policies   Spring

  _____ 2. Communicate with community leaders regularly,
              visit headquarters

  _____ 3. Invite community leaders/supervisors to
              visit the school

  _____ 4. Plan recruiting efforts   Winter

  _____ 5. Publicly recognize the contribution (past
              and present) of the religious community(ies)
              to the school

II. Board Policies

* _____ 1. Clarify contractual arrangements with the
              community or with individual religious   Spring

* _____ 2. Approve job conditions for religious personnel
              (salary, benefits, housing, auto, insurance, etc.) Spring

III. Faculty Handbook

  _____ 1. Recognize the history and traditions of the
              religious community(ies) serving in the school

IV. Parent/Student Handbook

_____ 1. Describe the history and tradition of the
          religious community

V. Helpful Resources

_____ 1. Religious community newsletter and publications

_____ 2. Planning for Catholic Education. NCEA Papers, Series II,
          No. 2. Washington, D.C.: National Catholic Educational
          Association

_____ 3. Retirement Programs for Religious in the U.S. Washington, D.C.:
          National Catholic Educational Association, 1977

VI. Issues

_____ 1. To what degree can we plan on religious personnel in
          Catholic schools in the future?

_____ 2. What are the distinctive contributions made by religious
          to Catholic schools?

_____ 3. What is the special challenge facing a lay principal of
          a school where there are religious on the staff?

_____ 4. Should religious receive salaries equivalent to those of
          lay teachers?

_____ 5. How can a Catholic school play a significant role in
          fostering religious vocations?

13. THE PRINCIPAL AND THE LAW

Although the legal requirements binding Catholic schools differ from state to state, all schools are subject to state law in some way, as well as to federal regulations affecting all American schools. It is up to the school principal to keep him/herself informed on current school law as it affects local Catholic schools, and to be the prime source of information for faculty and board members. For specific matters, it is recommended that a principal consult appropriate officials in the diocesan education office, the state Catholic conference, private school administrator associations, as well as local lawyers who are knowledgeable about legal matters affecting private schools. It is also incumbent upon Catholic school administrators to be a model of respect for existing law, and active in efforts to remove legal requirements which are unncecessary or unreasonable.

I. Administrative Actions to Take   Season

    *_____1. Know and carry out federal, state, and local
          laws which apply to Catholic schools

    _____2. Review pertinent laws with faculty at the
          beginning of school year   Fall

    _____3. Be aware of the laws and regulations
          applicable to local public schools

    *_____4. Keep accurate records as required by law

    *_____5. Keep the board informed of applicable
          legal requirements

II. Board Policies and Decisions   Season

     *_____1. Have non-discrimination policy renewed yearly   Fall

     *_____2. Secure knowledgeable legal advisor

     *_____3. Fulfill other local legal requirements
               applicable to boards

III. Faculty Handbook

     *_____1. Summary of legal requirements applicable
               to faculty

      _____2. Philosophy statement regarding the teacher
               as citizen role-model for the students

IV. Parent/Student Handbook

     *_____1. Lisiting of applicable laws regarding student
               conduct, student rights, student records,
               medications, absences, drug, tobacco, and
               alcohol, etc.

     *_____2. Access to and privacy of student records

V. Helpful Resources

      _____1. Diocesan offices

      _____2. State Catholic conferences

      _____3. Bulletins and publications of: National Catholic Educational
               Association, Council for American Private Education, local and
               state associations of private school administrators; United
               States Catholic Conference, Representative for Federal Assist-
               ance, 1312 Massachusetts Avenue, NW, Washington, DC 20005

_____ 4. Publications on school law intended for public school use may be helpful, but must be used with care because of the important differences in legal requirements on public and private schools

_____ 5. Legal Educational Services Report. Washington, D.C.: National Catholic Educational Association, Secondary Deparment, issued 6 times a year

_____ 6. Manno, Bruno V. How to Service Students with Federal Education Program Benefits. Washington, D.C.: National Catholic Educational Association, 1980

_____ 7. Permuth, Steve, Mawdsley, Ralph, and Daly, Joseph. School Law, Students, and Catholic Education. Washington, D.C.: National Catholic Educational Association, 1981

_____ 8. Private School Law Digest. Dayton, OH: University of Dayton, issued 6 times a year

VI. Issues

_____ 1. What laws definitely apply to private schools? Which ones do not? Which are ambiguous? How is a Catholic school principal to act in the case where application to the Catholic school is unclear?

_____ 2. How can liability suits be avoided in our present "sue-crazed" society?

_____ 3. How do we observe copyright laws with fairness to authors and publishers?

_____ 4. How are faculty and student rights protected and the common welfare of the school served at the same time?

_____ 5. What are effective grievance procedures for faculty, parents, and students?

_____ 6. What are censorship rights of a school principal with regard to school publications?

14. THE PRINCIPAL AND GOVERNMENT AID TO NONPUBLIC STUDENTS

The principal of a private school has the responsiblity for knowing and administering the programs of aid available to nonpublic students from government sources. The principal is also an important leader for informing and motivating parents in the campaign for such programs.

I. Administrative Actions to Take   Season

    *_____1. Knows all current programs which are available

    *_____2. Fulfills requirements (records, reports, etc.)

    *_____3. Maintains contact with diocesan and local
           public school coordinators of nonpublic aid
           programs

    _____4. Reviews programs for the coming year   Spring

    _____5. Sets procedure for resolving questions and
           problems regarding aid   Summer

    _____6. Is an active member of Citizens for Educational
           Freedom and/or other parent advocacy groups

    _____7. Informs parents of current efforts to expand
           (or deny) aid to nonpublic students

II. Board Policies and Actions

    *_____1. Approves the extent of the school's participation
           in aid programs

    _____2. Supports efforts to expand aid

III. Faculty Handbook

    *_____1. Teacher responsibilibites regarding government
           aid programs.

_____2. Encouragement to participate in advocacy efforts (CEF)

IV. Parent/Student Handbook

_____1. Summary of government aid programs available in the schools

_____2. Encouragement to be involved in advocacy groups (CEF)

V. Helpful Resources

_____1. Blum, Rev. Virgil, S.J. Catholic Parents: Political Eunchs.
St. Cloud, MN: Media Materials, 1972

_____2. Manno, Bruno V. How to Service Students with Federal Education
Program Benefits. Washington, D.C.: National Catholic Educational
Association, 1980

_____3. Private Schools: Fact and Future. Washington, D.C.: Council
for American Private Education, 1976

_____4. Tavel, David. Church-State Issues in Education. Bloomington,
IN: Phi Delta Kappa, 1979

_____5. also, consult the following:
Citizens for Educational Freedom, Washington Building, Suite 854, 15th
& New York Avenue, NW, Washington, DC 20005
Council for American Private Education (CAPE), 1625 Eye St., NW,
Washington, DC 20006
Diocesan Education Office
State Catholic Conferences

VI. Issues

_____1. At what point are the benefits of an aid program outweighed by
the time, work, and controls it brings?

_____2. Do private schools surrender their independence by accepting
aid for their students?

_____3. Can a principal delegate the responsibility for administering
government programs?

15. THE PRINCIPAL AND PUBLIC RELATIONS

Catholic schools have shifted from a "seller's market", where applications outnumbered available spaces, to the present "buyer's market", when declining births and greater parent selectivity have forced Catholic school principals into the realm of "marketing" their institutions so as to continue to attract students. The need for a definite informational and promotional program has become clear. Such activities are also necessary to attract the financial resources needed for the operation of Catholic schools.

I. <u>Administrative Actions to Take</u>   Season

    *_____1. Plan external communication tools: Spring and
            newsletter, brochure, parish bulletin   Summer
            inserts, handbooks

    _____2. Plan annual public relations program   Summer

    *_____3. Plan recruiting program   Fall

    _____4. Make contact with local media personnel
            and maintain communication with them

    _____5. Plan American Education Week and Catholic   Fall and
            School Week observances   Winter

    _____6. Place school registration information
            with local realtors

    _____7. Appoint Public Relations Coordinator

II. <u>Board Policies and Decisions</u>

    _____1. Assist as appropriate in school public
            relations program

    *_____2. Approve policy for recruitment and admission
            of children of non-parishioners and of
            non-Catholic children   Fall

III. <u>Faculty Handbook</u>

    _____1. Summary of faculty involvement in public relations program

    _____2. Faculty assistance in recruiting program

    *_____3. List of public relations and recuriting events planned for the year

    _____4. Encouragement to suggest publicity items to school public relations coordinator

IV. <u>Parent/Student Handbook</u>

    _____1. Appeal to assist in school recruiting program

    *_____2. Name of radio station which will carry school-closing announcements and other emergency information

V. <u>Resources</u>

    _____1. Glenzinski, Mary, and Harrington, Rev. Emmit. <u>The Principal's Toolbox</u>. Washington, D.C.: National Catholic Educational Association, 1975

    _____2. Hillman, Sheilah. <u>Public Relations for Private Schools</u>. San Francisco: Institute for Catholic Educational Leadership, University of San Francisco School of Education, 1976

    _____3. Byrne, Robert, and Powell, Edward. <u>Strengthening School and Community Relations</u>. Reston, Virginia: National Association of Secondary School Principals, 1976

    _____4. Catholic School Week kits, available from NCEA. (These are published each year with emphasis upon the theme of the year; however, much of the material is helpful for a continuing public relations program for Catholic schools.)

    _____5. National School Public Relations Association publications (1801 North Moore Street, Washington, D.C. 22209)

VI. <u>Issues</u>

_____1. To what extent do principles of commercial marketing apply to public relations and recruiting for Catholic schools?

_____2. How can effective public relations rectify false expectations which the public may have of Catholic schools?

_____3. What is the best way to find out what the public thinks of your school?

_____4. How should a principal respond to negative publicity for his/her school?

_____5. Is it possible to have too much public relations?

_____6. What percent of the principal's time should be spent on public relations?

_____7. How can parents and students be involved in recruiting?

_____8. Should Catholic schools compete with each other for students?

_____9. How can recruiting be effective without reflecting unfavorably upon "competing" Catholic and public schools?

16. THE PRINCIPAL AND EVALUATION

Education is often said to be a process which can be carried on as it has been in the past, with no real regard for the results achieved. For this reason, school administrators are unfavorably compared with business people; the latter are always concerned with the "bottom line" and are able to see very tangible results of their efforts in terms of profit or loss. However, education deals with the intangible, and results cannot be described with the accuracy of monetary loss and gain; nevertheless, it belongs to the integrity of school administrators that they use all the means possible to measure what they are doing and how they are doing it - for the maximum benefit of the pupils they serve, as well as to be accountable to the public whose resources they are using for the operation of Catholic schools. The limited funds available to Catholic school leaders make this accountability all the more necessary.

It is important that evaluation deals with (1) students, (2) faculty, (3) the administrator him/herself, and (4) the school in general as an organization. This evaluation must deal both with process (how things are done) and with product (what is the result).

I. Administrative Actions to Take		Season
*_____ 1. Select tools to evaluate:		Spring and Summer
_____ a. students		
_____ b. teachers		
_____ c. principal		
_____ d. school		
_____ e. board		

*_____2. Select means of reporting evaluation
         when completed

*_____3. Decide on follow-up indicated as a result
         of the various evaluations

_____4. Publicize testing results with discretion

*_____5. Initiate or continue accredition of the
         school if desirable

*_____6. Work out a schedule for the various
         evaluation activities

*_____7. Involve staff and board in the evaluation
         process as may be appropriate

_____8. Inform board of evaluation results of
         students, teachers, school

II. Board Policies and Decisions

*_____1. Decide on principal evaluation process

_____2. Decide on application for accreditation

*_____3. Approve policy on promotion and
         graduation

III. Faculty Handbook

*_____1. Teacher evaluation process

*_____2. Student testing and reporting procedures

_____3. School evaluation process

_____4. Accreditiation requirements

IV. Parent/Student Handbook

*_____1. Nature of school's accreditation

*_____2. Student testing program

*_____3. Schedule of parent-teacher conferences
            and report cards

*_____4. Requirements for promotion and graduation

V. Resources

_____1. Publications of the National Catholic Educational Association:

          The Qualities and Competencies of the Religion Teacher
          Criteria for the Evaluation of Religious Education Programs
          The Religious Education Outcomes Inventory
          Religious Education Knowledge, Attitudes, and Practice
          The Principal's Toolbox
          Guidelines for Selected Personnel Practices in Catholic Schools (I)
          Giving Form to the Vision (available in four sections: Adult,
              Elementary, Secondary, Policy-Making)
          Evaluation of Religious Formation Programs

_____2. Publications of the regional accrediting associations, of the
          Independent Schools Association of the Central States, and of
          the Jesuit Secondary Education Association

_____3. Evaluation plans published by diocesan offices

_____4. Elford, George. The Catholic School in Theory and Practice.
          Washington, D.C.: National Catholic Educational Association, 1973

VI. Issues

_____1. To what degree is it possible to evaluate the results of
          education?

_____2. What are the uses and abuses of standardized tests?

_____3. What is the principal's responsibility regarding evaluation
          of teachers?

_____4. What information from student and teacher evaluation should be
          released to the board, to parents, to faculty, to the public?

_____5. How should administrators be evaluated?

_____6. Should nonprofessionals (i.e., the board) evaluate the principal?
          How?